The Zen of Dogs

Wisdom That Wags the Tail

LAINE CUNNINGHAM

The Zen of Dogs
Wisdom That Wags the Tail

Published by Sun Dogs Creations
Changing the World One Book at a Time
Softcover ISBN: 9781946732316
Hardcover ISBN: 9781946732323

Softcover Edition

Cover Design by Angel Leya

Copyright © 2017 and 2019 Laine Cunningham

All rights reserved. No part of this book may be reproduced in any form or by any means, electronic, mechanical, digital, photocopying or recording, except for the inclusion in a review, without permission in writing from the publisher.

Introduction

Dogs have always enriched my life. Our family's first dachshund was named Dino after a cartoon dinosaur. Dino I was followed by two other dachshunds...Dino II and Dino III, naturally. Then came a snaggletoothed champagne poodle.

Once I struck out on my own, I rescued an anxious Chow-Cocker Spaniel mix, an angelic Shepherd-Rottweiler mix, a purebred Doberman named Scooby, and a Chesapeake Bay Retriever who even now is snoozing in my studio.

Each of these dogs provided friendship and a generous, boundless love. Their trusting natures forgave my every misstep. Their hearts remained always open. On bad days and good, their playfulness and the relaxed ease that belongs only to a dog enriched my life.

This collection of unique sayings shares the wisdom discovered while living with these special companions. Everyone deserves the precious gift that is *The Zen of Dogs*.

Never catching a squirrel doesn't end the chase.

Biscuits last a moment.
Loyalty lasts a lifetime.

Meet someone new and your pack grows bigger.

A slobbery chew toy is a
gateway to nirvana.

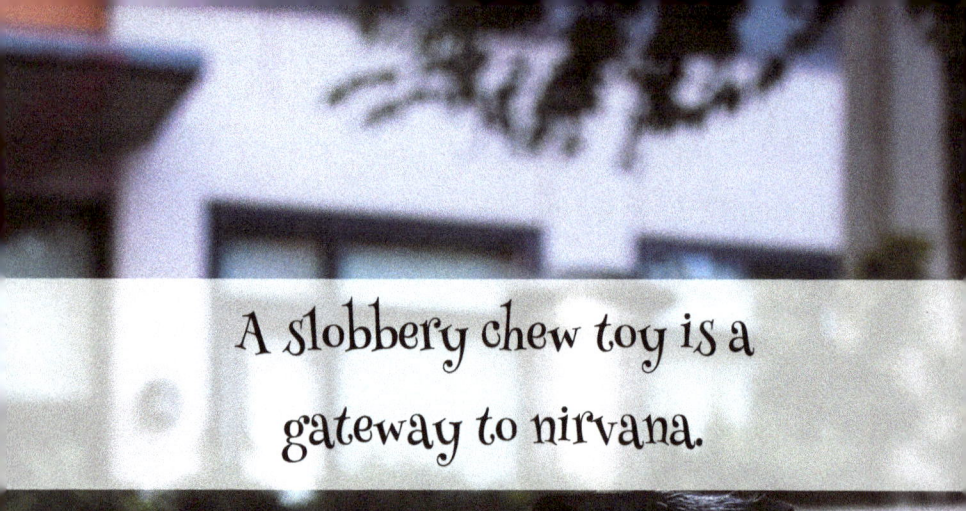

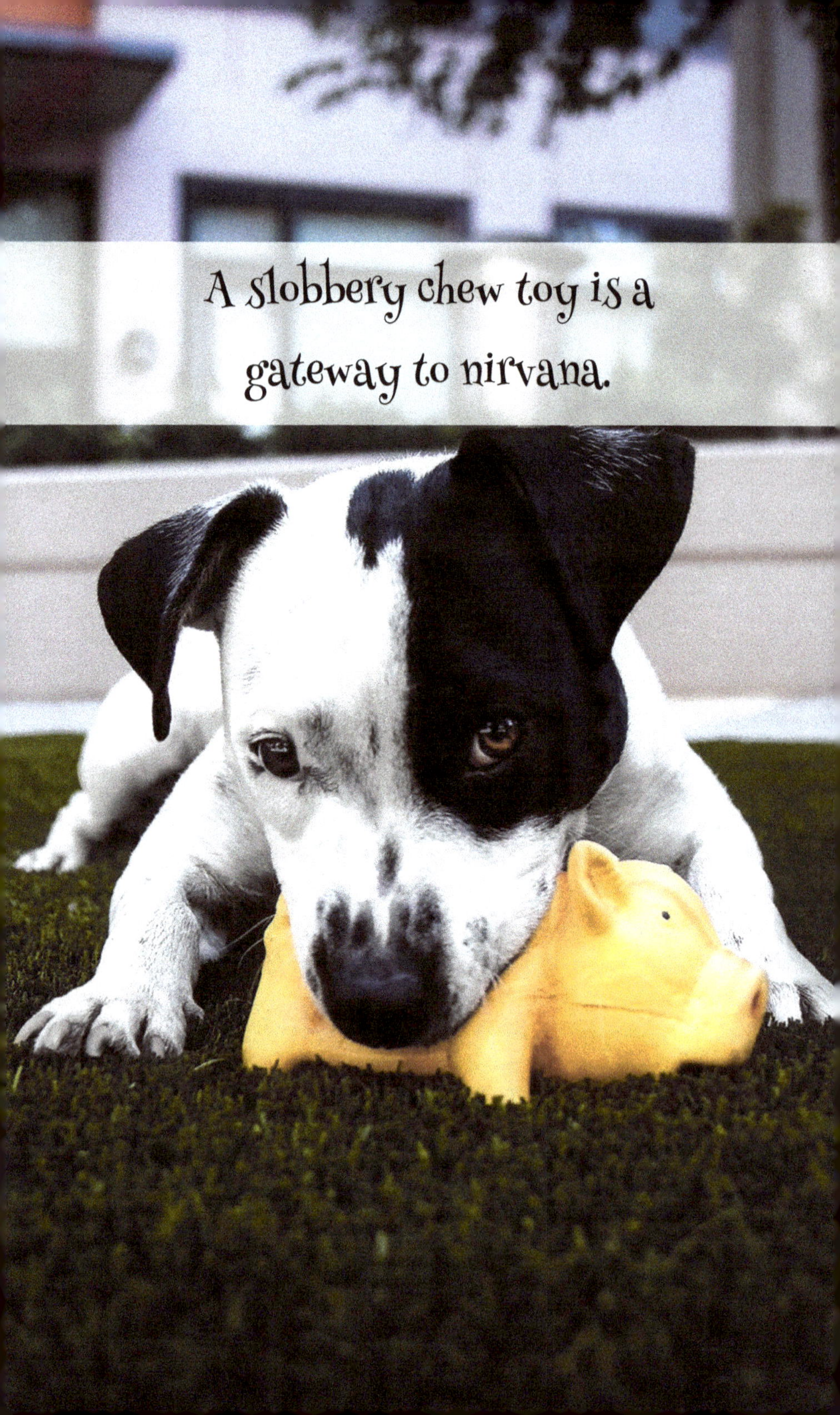

Hunting is not a solo activity.

The joy of Frisbee is the joy of total focus.

Greetings should always be exuberant.

Leftovers are the best part of the meal.

An all-over shake resets your attitude.

A well-timed leap snags the ball.

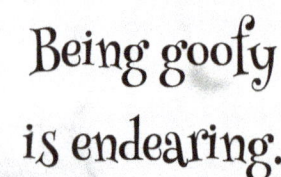

Being goofy is endearing.

The present moment is the only one that counts.

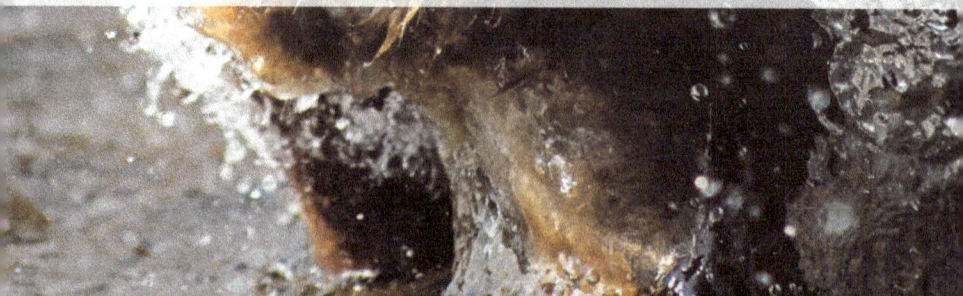

All living beings must run free.

A house that shelters a dog is a home sheltered by love.

Dogs evolved alongside us.
We evolved alongside dogs.

A world without dogs would nurture only wolves.

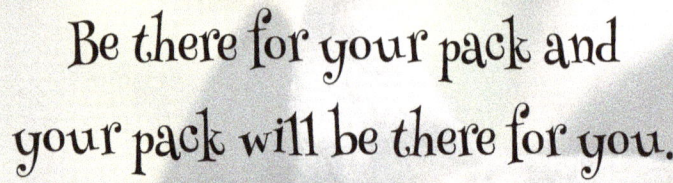

Be there for your pack and your pack will be there for you.

Life is a full-body experience.

Despite their size, fleas are a torment.

Howling is best in the company of friends.

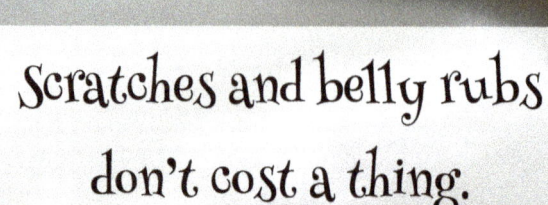

Scratches and belly rubs don't cost a thing.

The sense of smell is entirely underappreciated.

Lassie was a real dog.
Every dog is Lassie.

The pure heart remains open.

Play is the linchpin of life.

Your domain encompasses everything you see.

Greet your loved ones every time they come home.

There are no bad smells.
There are only weak noses.

Your purpose is embedded in your pack.

Exercise judgment but never be judgmental.

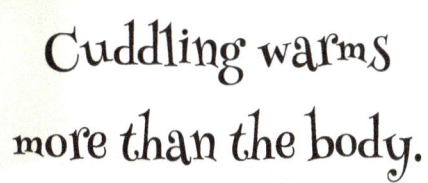

Cuddling warms more than the body.

Never disguise your happiness.

Fretting over an empty bowl does not fill it with food.

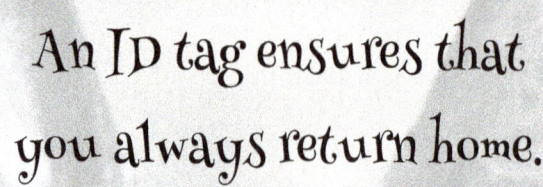

An ID tag ensures that you always return home.

Food, family and fun are the building blocks of life.

Life cannot be lived at the end of a chain.

Growling settles disputes before the fight begins.

A snooze in the sunshine refreshes body and mind.

A collar can be fancy but really, who cares?

Marking your territory sets boundaries for others.

What you chase doesn't matter as long as you chase something.

About the Author

Laine Cunningham's books take readers on adventures around the world. *The Family Made of Dust* is set in the Australian Outback, while *Reparation* is a novel of the American Great Plains. Her women's travel adventure memoir *Woman Alone: A Six-Month Journey Through the Australian Outback* appeals to fans of *Wild* and *Eat Pray Love*. Her work has received multiple awards including the Hackney and the James Jones Fellowship, and has been published by *Reed*, *Birmingham Arts Journal*, and the annual anthology by *Writer's Digest*. She is the senior editor of *Sunspot Literary Journal*.

Fiction

The Family Made of Dust
Beloved
Reparation

Nonfiction

Woman Alone
On the Wallaby Track: Australian Words and Phrases
Seven Sisters: Messages from Aboriginal Australia
Writing While Female or Black or Gay
The Wisdom of Puppies
The Wisdom of Babies
The Wisdom of Weddings

The Zen of Travel
The Zen of Gardening
Zen in the Stable
The Zen of Chocolate
The Zen of Dogs

Bikes of Berlin
Necropolises of New Orleans I & II
Ruins of Rome I & II
Ancients of Assisi I & II
Panoramas of Portugal
Nuances of New York
Glimpses of Germany
Impressions of Italy
Altitudes of the Alps
Knights Through the Ages
Utopia of the Unicorn
Portraits of Paris
Flourishes of France

www.ingramcontent.com/pod-product-compliance
Lightning Source LLC
Chambersburg PA
CBHW041959080526
44588CB00021B/2806